easy

Tapas

easy

Tapas

Love Food ® is an imprint of Parragon Books Ltd

Parragon
Queen Street House
4 Queen Street
Bath BA1 1HE, UK

ISBN: 978-1-4075-5437-2

Printed in China

Introduction by Susanna Tee
Additional photography by Clive Streeter
Additional food styling by Angela Drake

NOTES FOR THE READER
This book uses both metric and imperial measurements. Follow the same units of measurement
throughout; do not mix metric and imperial. All spoon measurements are level: teaspoons are
assumed to be 5 ml, and tablespoons are assumed to be 15 ml. Unless otherwise stated, milk is
assumed to be full fat, eggs and individual vegetables are medium, and pepper is freshly ground
black pepper.

Recipes using raw or very lightly cooked eggs should be avoided by infants, the elderly, pregnant
women, convalescents and anyone suffering from an illness. Pregnant and breastfeeding women are
advised to avoid eating peanuts and peanut products. Sufferers from nut allergies should be aware
that some of the ready-made ingredients used in the recipes in this book may contain nuts. Always
check the packaging before use.

Contents

Introduction

Tapas, those little tempting morsels of food, are found on almost every bar counter in Spain. Eating them, accompanied with a glass of dry sherry, chilled white wine or a beer, before lunch or dinner, is a part of everyday Spanish life. It is an informal way of eating and, in Spain, the tapas experience accompanies friendship and conversation. There is even the Spanish tradition of *el tapeo*, or 'eating tapas', when friends stroll from one bar to another, customarily standing, talking, drinking and sampling the house specialities of each.

The History of Tapas

The Spanish word 'tapa' means a 'lid' or 'cover' and it is from Andalusia that the most commonly cited explanation originates. It is thought that Andalusian innkeepers put a slice of bread on top of glasses of sherry or wine to keep out the fruit flies and dust between sips. This led to the addition of a slice of ham or cheese to make it a snack and then to more elaborate toppings to attract customers, and hence tapas were created.

The Culinary Repertoire

The variety of ingredients and dishes, both hot and cold, that make up tapas are enormous. There are, of course, delicious combinations piled on bread or toast. In addition, there are fried vegetables and fish, meatballs, croquettes, fritters, omelettes, tapas on cocktail sticks and ingredients cooked in a sauce. It is also rare not to include one or two types of olives as well as crusty bread to eat with sauce-based tapas. Bowls of salted almonds, chunks of Manchego cheese and chorizo sausage are always popular. Vegetables, particularly tomatoes, aubergines, peppers and potatoes, fresh meat and poultry, cured meats, dairy produce and usually one or more fish or shellfish are all part of this culinary experience.

Serving Tapas

Tapas have now evolved into an entire cuisine, and in cafés, restaurants and the home, a selection of these delicious miniature morsels can be a meal in themselves. For an informal lunch or supper party, serve about six different types of tapas dishes, choosing your selection from the different chapters in this book. Select a variety of hot and cold tapas and include a selection of simple tapas, such as bowls of olives, almonds, cheese and chorizo sausage. These simple tapas are also ideal to serve with pre-dinner drinks.

Tapas dishes are the perfect, easy dish to serve as a starter at a dinner party or as a light lunch dish. In these instances, halve the number of servings that the recipe suggests it serves and accompany with Spanish bread and a salad. In addition, tapas are ideal for serving at an informal party. Allow eight to ten servings per person and multiply quantities of the recipes as necessary. For these occasions, you will find that not only are the recipes easy to prepare but they can also be prepared in advance.

Essential Ingredients

Almonds A bowl of blanched almonds is one of the easiest tapas to make. For freshness, buy unblanched almonds and blanch just before using – just drop the nuts into boiling water for a few minutes, then drain and refresh under cold water. Use your fingers to squeeze the nuts so they pop out of their skins.

Cheese For a typical tapas ingredient, keep the traditional Manchego cheese, a sheep's milk cheese from La Mancha, and cubes of Cabrales, a rich blue cheese, to serve with drinks.

Cured Meats Serrano or mountain ham, perhaps the best known, features at many tapas bars – it can be served in thin slices, as sandwich filling or on bread topped with vegetables. The most highly regarded cured hams are labelled as Iberico and can be identified by the hefty price! Other popular cured meats are pork loin and Spain's ubiquitous pork sausage – the spicy chorizo.

Garlic An essential Spanish flavouring. Buy fresh and use within a month once the head has been broken into.

Olive Oil Olive oil is a regular feature of Spanish cooking. Heat destroys the flavour of oil so save your best extra virgin oil for uncooked dishes and cook with plain olive oil.

Paprika Made from ground, dried red peppers, paprika adds a mild or strong smoky flavour and vibrant red colour to dishes.

Pulses Spanish kitchen cupboards contain many jars and cans of pulses, cooked and ready to use without first having to go to the trouble of overnight soaking and boiling.

Canned Fish There is a wide selection of canned fish available, including anchovies, sardines and tuna. Buy fish preserved in oil for the best flavour.

1

Little Bites

Cracked Marinated Olives

serves 8

450 g/1 lb can or jar unstoned large green olives, drained

4 garlic cloves, peeled

2 tsp coriander seeds

1 small lemon

4 sprigs of fresh thyme

4 feathery stalks of fennel

2 small fresh red chillies (optional)

extra virgin olive oil

pepper

To allow the flavours of the marinade to penetrate the olives, place the olives on a chopping board and, using a rolling pin, bash them lightly so that they crack slightly. Alternatively, use a sharp knife to cut a lengthways slit in each olive as far as the stone. Using the flat side of a broad knife, lightly crush each garlic clove. Using a pestle and mortar, crack the coriander seeds. Cut the lemon, with its rind, into small chunks.

Put the olives, garlic, coriander seeds, lemon chunks, thyme sprigs, fennel and chillies, if using, in a large bowl and toss together. Season with pepper to taste, but you should not need to add salt as conserved olives are usually salty enough. Pack the ingredients tightly into a glass jar with a lid. Pour in enough olive oil to cover the olives, then seal the jar tightly.

Leave the olives at room temperature for 24 hours, then marinate in the refrigerator for at least 1 week but preferably 2 weeks before serving. From time to time, gently give the jar a shake to re-mix the ingredients. Return the olives to room temperature and remove from the oil to serve. Provide cocktail sticks for spearing the olives.

Olives with Orange & Lemon

serves 4–6

2 tsp fennel seeds

2 tsp cumin seeds

225 g/8 oz green Spanish olives

225 g/8 oz black Spanish olives

2 tsp grated orange rind

2 tsp grated lemon rind

3 shallots, finely chopped

pinch of ground cinnamon

4 tbsp white wine vinegar

5 tbsp Spanish extra virgin olive oil

2 tbsp orange juice

1 tbsp fresh mint, chopped

1 tbsp fresh parsley, chopped

Dry-fry the fennel seeds and cumin seeds in a small, heavy-based frying pan, shaking the pan frequently, until they begin to pop and give off their aroma. Remove the frying pan from the heat and leave to cool.

Place the olives, orange rind and lemon rind, shallots, cinnamon and toasted seeds in a bowl.

Whisk the vinegar, olive oil, orange juice, mint and parsley together in a bowl and pour over the olives. Toss well, cover and leave to chill for 1–2 days before serving.

Salted Almonds

serves 6

225 g/8 oz whole almonds, blanched

4 tbsp Spanish olive oil

coarse sea salt

1 tsp paprika or ground cumin (optional)

Preheat the oven to 180°C/350°F/Gas Mark 4. Place the olive oil in a roasting tin and swirl it around so that it covers the base. Add the almonds and toss them in the tin so that they are evenly coated in the oil, then spread them out in a single layer.

Roast the almonds in the preheated oven for 20 minutes, or until they are light golden brown, tossing several times during the cooking. Drain the almonds on kitchen paper, then transfer them to a bowl.

While the almonds are still warm, sprinkle with plenty of sea salt and paprika, if using, and toss together to coat. Serve the almonds warm or cold. The almonds are at their best when served freshly cooked, so, if possible, cook them on the day that you plan to eat them. However, they can be stored in an airtight container for up to 3 days.

Sautéed Garlic Mushrooms

serves 6

450 g/1 lb button mushrooms

5 tbsp olive oil

2 garlic cloves, finely chopped

squeeze of lemon juice

4 tbsp fresh flat-leaf parsley, chopped, plus extra sprigs to garnish

salt and pepper

crusty bread, to serve

Wipe or brush clean the mushrooms, then trim off the stalks close to the caps. Cut any large mushrooms in half or into quarters. Heat the olive oil in a large, heavy-based frying pan, add the garlic and fry for 30 seconds–1 minute, or until lightly browned. Add the mushrooms and sauté over a high heat, stirring most of the time, until the mushrooms have absorbed all the oil in the pan.

Reduce the heat to low. When the juices have come out of the mushrooms, increase the heat again and sauté for 4–5 minutes, stirring most of the time, until the juices have almost evaporated. Add a squeeze of lemon juice and season to taste with salt and pepper. Stir in the parsley and cook for a further minute.

Transfer the sautéed mushrooms to a warmed serving dish and serve piping hot or warm, garnished with the parsley sprigs. Accompany with chunks or slices of crusty bread for mopping up the garlic cooking juices.

Patatas Bravas

serves 6

1 kg/2 lb 4 oz potatoes

salt

Spanish olive oil,
for shallow-frying

for the sauce

1 onion, finely chopped

2 garlic cloves, crushed

50 ml/2 fl oz white wine or
dry Spanish sherry

400 g/14 oz canned
chopped tomatoes

2 tsp white or red
wine vinegar

1–2 tsp crushed dried
chillies

2 tsp hot or sweet smoked
Spanish paprika

To make the sauce, heat 2 tablespoons of oil in a saucepan, add the onion and cook over a medium heat, stirring occasionally, for 5 minutes, or until softened but not browned. Add the garlic and cook, stirring, for 30 seconds. Add the wine and bring to the boil. Add the tomatoes, vinegar, chillies and paprika, reduce the heat and simmer, uncovered, for 10–15 minutes until a thick sauce forms.

When the sauce is cooked, put into a food processor or blender and process until smooth. Return the sauce to the saucepan and set aside.

Do not peel the potatoes, but cut them into chunky pieces. Heat enough oil in a large frying pan to come about 2.5 cm/ 1 inch up the side of the pan. Add the potato pieces and cook over a medium–high heat, turning occasionally, for 10–15 minutes until golden brown. Remove with a slotted spoon, drain on kitchen paper and sprinkle with salt.

Meanwhile, gently reheat the sauce. Transfer the potatoes to a warmed serving dish and drizzle over the sauce. Serve hot, with wooden cocktail sticks to spear the potatoes.

Baby Potatoes with Aïoli

serves 6–8

450 g/1 lb baby new potatoes

ready-made aïoli, to coat

1 tbsp fresh parsley, chopped

salt

To prepare the potatoes, cut them in half or quarters to make bite-sized pieces. If they are very small, you can leave them whole. Put the potatoes in a large saucepan of cold, salted water and bring to the boil. Reduce the heat and simmer for 7 minutes, or until just tender. Drain well, then turn out into a large bowl.

While the potatoes are still warm, pour over the aïoli sauce, to coat, and gently toss the potatoes in it. Adding the sauce to the potatoes while they are still warm will help them to absorb the garlic flavour. Leave for about 20 minutes to allow the potatoes to marinate in the sauce.

Transfer the potatoes with aïoli to a warmed serving dish, sprinkle over the parsley and salt to taste and serve warm. Alternatively, the dish can be prepared ahead and stored in the refrigerator, but return it to room temperature before serving.

Potato & Spinach Triangles

serves 4

2 tbsp butter, melted, plus extra for greasing

225 g/8 oz waxy potatoes, finely diced

500 g/1 lb 2 oz fresh baby spinach

2 tbsp water

1 tomato, deseeded and chopped

¼ tsp chilli powder

½ tsp lemon juice

225 g/8 oz (8 sheets) filo pastry, thawed if frozen

salt and pepper

Preheat the oven to 190°C/375°F/Gas Mark 5. Lightly grease a baking tray with a little butter. Cook the potatoes in a saucepan of lightly salted boiling water for 10 minutes, or until tender. Drain thoroughly and place in a mixing bowl.

Meanwhile, put the spinach into a large saucepan with the water, cover and cook, stirring occasionally, over a low heat for 2 minutes, or until wilted. Drain the spinach thoroughly, squeezing out the excess moisture, and add to the potatoes. Stir in the tomato, chilli powder and lemon juice. Season to taste with salt and pepper.

Lightly brush the sheets of filo pastry with melted butter. Spread out 4 of the sheets and lay a second sheet on top of each. Cut them into rectangles about 20 x 10 cm/ 8 x 4 inches.

Spoon a portion of the potato and spinach mixture onto one end of each rectangle. Fold a corner of the pastry over the filling, fold the pointed end back over the pastry strip, then fold over the remaining pastry to form a triangle.

Place the triangles on the prepared baking tray and bake in the preheated oven for 20 minutes, or until golden brown. Serve hot or cold.

Tapenade

serves 4

100 g/3½ oz canned anchovy fillets

350 g/12 oz black olives, stoned and coarsely chopped

2 garlic cloves, coarsely chopped

2 tbsp capers, drained and rinsed

1 tbsp Dijon mustard

3 tbsp extra virgin olive oil

2 tbsp lemon juice

Drain the anchovies, reserving the oil from the can. Coarsely chop the fish and place into a food processor or blender. Add the reserved oil and all the remaining ingredients. Process to a smooth purée. Stop and scrape down the sides if necessary.

Transfer the tapenade to a dish, cover with clingfilm and chill in the refrigerator until required. If you are not planning to use the tapenade until the following day (or even the one after), cover the surface with a layer of olive oil to prevent it from drying out.

Fresh Mint & Bean Pâté

serves 12

800 g/1 lb 12 oz fresh broad beans in their pods, shelled to give about 350 g/12 oz

225 g/8 oz soft goat's cheese

1 garlic clove, crushed

2 spring onions, finely chopped

1 tbsp Spanish extra virgin olive oil, plus extra to serve

grated rind of 1 lemon and 2 tbsp lemon juice

about 60 large fresh mint leaves, about 15 g/½ oz in total

12 slices of baguette

salt and pepper

Cook the broad beans in a saucepan of boiling water for 8–10 minutes until tender. Drain well and leave to cool. When the beans are cool enough to handle, slip off their skins and put them in a food processor or blender.

Add the goat's cheese, garlic, spring onions, oil, lemon rind and lemon juice and mint leaves to the broad beans and process until well mixed. Season the pâté to taste with salt and pepper. Turn into a bowl, cover and chill in the refrigerator for at least 1 hour before serving.

To serve, preheat the grill to high. Toast the baguette slices under the grill until golden brown on both sides. Drizzle a little oil over the toasted bread slices, spread the pâté on top and serve immediately.

Simmered Summer Vegetables

serves 6–8

1 large aubergine

4 tbsp Spanish olive oil

1 onion, thinly sliced

2 garlic cloves, finely chopped

2 courgettes, thinly sliced

1 red pepper, cored, deseeded and thinly sliced

1 green pepper, cored, deseeded and thinly sliced

8 tomatoes, peeled, deseeded and chopped

salt and pepper

fresh parsley, chopped, to garnish

slices thick country bread, to serve (optional)

Cut the aubergine into 2.5-cm/1-inch cubes. Heat the oil in a large flameproof casserole, add the onion and cook over a medium heat, stirring occasionally, for 5 minutes, or until softened but not browned. Add the garlic and cook, stirring, for 30 seconds until softened.

Increase the heat to medium–high, add the aubergine cubes and cook, stirring occasionally, for 10 minutes, or until softened and beginning to brown. Add the courgettes and peppers and cook, stirring occasionally, for 10 minutes until softened. Add the tomatoes and season to taste with salt and pepper.

Bring the mixture to the boil, then reduce the heat, cover and simmer, stirring occasionally so that the vegetables do not stick to the base of the pan, for 15–20 minutes until tender. If necessary, uncover, increase the heat and cook to evaporate any excess liquid, as the mixture should be thick.

Serve hot or cold, garnished with chopped parsley and accompanied by bread slices for scooping up the vegetables, if desired.

Broad Bean Salad

serves 4

2.5 kg/5 lb 8 oz fresh broad beans in their pods or 425 g/15 oz frozen broad beans

2 tomatoes, peeled, deseeded and diced

3 tbsp basil, shredded

50 g/1¾ oz Parmesan shavings

for the dressing

1 tsp white wine vinegar

1 small garlic clove, crushed

4 tbsp extra virgin olive oil

salt and pepper

Bring a large pan of water to the boil. If using fresh broad beans, shell them and rinse under cold water. Add the beans to the pan, bring back to the boil, then cook for 3 minutes, until just tender. Drain and tip into a serving dish or arrange on individual plates.

Whisk the dressing ingredients together and spoon it over the beans while still warm.

Scatter over the tomatoes, basil and Parmesan shavings. Serve immediately, at room temperature in a warmed bowl.

Spicy Tomato Salad

serves 4

4 large ripe tomatoes
1 small fresh red chilli
1 garlic clove
25 g/1 oz fresh basil
4 tbsp extra virgin olive oil
1 tbsp lemon juice
2 tbsp balsamic vinegar
salt and pepper
fresh basil sprigs, to garnish
fresh crusty bread, to serve

Bring a kettle of water to the boil. Place the tomatoes in a heatproof bowl, then pour over enough boiling water to cover them. Let them soak for 2–4 minutes, then lift out of the water and leave to cool slightly.

When the tomatoes are cool enough to handle, gently pierce the skins with the point of a knife. The skins should now be easy to remove. Discard the skins, then chop the tomatoes and place them in a large salad bowl.

Deseed and finely chop the chilli, then chop the garlic. Rinse and finely chop the basil, then add it to the tomatoes in the bowl with the chilli and the garlic.

Mix the oil, lemon juice and balsamic vinegar together in a separate bowl, then season to taste with salt and pepper. Pour the mixture over the salad and toss together well. Garnish with basil sprigs and serve immediately with fresh crusty bread.

Stuffed Cherry Tomatoes

serves 8

24 cherry tomatoes

for the anchovy & olive filling

50 g/1¾ oz canned anchovy fillets in olive oil

8 pimiento-stuffed green Spanish olives, finely chopped

2 large hard-boiled eggs, finely chopped

pepper

for the crab filling

170 g/6 oz canned crabmeat, drained

4 tbsp mayonnaise

1 tbsp fresh parsley, chopped

salt and pepper

paprika, to garnish

for the olive & caper filling

12 stoned black Spanish olives

3 tbsp capers

6 tbsp aïoli

salt and pepper

If necessary, cut and discard a very thin slice from the stalk end of each tomato to make the bases flat and stable. Cut a thin slice from the smooth end of each cherry tomato and discard. Using a serrated knife or teaspoon, loosen the pulp and seeds of each and scoop out, discarding the flesh. Turn the scooped-out tomatoes upside down on kitchen paper and leave to drain for 5 minutes.

To make the anchovy and olive filling, drain the anchovies, reserving the olive oil for later, then chop finely and place in a bowl. Add the olives and hard-boiled eggs. Pour in a trickle of the reserved olive oil to moisten the mixture, then season with pepper. Don't add salt to season as the anchovies are salty. Mix well together.

To make the crab filling, place the crabmeat, mayonnaise and parsley in a bowl and mix well together. Season the filling to taste with salt and pepper. Sprinkle with paprika before serving.

To make the olive and caper filling, place the olives and capers on kitchen paper to drain them well, then chop finely and place in a bowl. Add the aïoli and mix well together. Season the filling to taste with salt and pepper.

Fill a piping bag fitted with a 2-cm/¾-inch plain nozzle with the filling of your choice and use to fill the hollow tomato shells. Store the cherry tomatoes in the refrigerator until ready to serve.

Pickled Stuffed Peppers

serves 6

200 g/7 oz cuajada cheese, queso del tietar or other fresh goat's cheese

400 g/14 oz pickled peppers or pimientos del piquillo, drained

1 tbsp fresh dill, finely chopped

salt and pepper

Cut the cheese into pieces about 1 cm/½ inch long. Slit the sides of the peppers and deseed, if you like. Stuff the peppers with the cheese.

Arrange the stuffed peppers on serving plates, sprinkle with the dill and season to taste with salt and pepper. Cover and chill until ready to serve.

Roasted Peppers & Tomatoes

serves 4

2 red peppers
2 yellow peppers
2 orange peppers
4 tomatoes, halved
1 tbsp olive oil
3 garlic cloves, chopped
1 onion, sliced in rings
2 tbsp fresh thyme
salt and pepper

Halve and deseed the peppers. Place them, cut-side down, on a baking tray and cook under a preheated grill for 10 minutes. Add the tomatoes to the baking tray and grill for 5 minutes, until the skins of the peppers and tomatoes are charred.

Put the peppers into a polythene bag for 10 minutes to sweat, which will make the skin easier to peel. Remove the tomato skins and chop the flesh. Peel the skins from the peppers and slice the flesh into strips.

Heat the oil in a large frying pan and fry the garlic and onion, stirring occasionally, for 3–4 minutes or until softened. Add the peppers and tomatoes to the frying pan and cook for 5 minutes. Stir in the fresh thyme and season to taste with salt and pepper.

Transfer to serving bowls and serve warm or chilled.

Courgette Fritters with a Dipping Sauce

serves 6–8

450 g/1 lb baby courgettes

3 tbsp plain flour

1 tsp paprika

1 large egg

2 tbsp milk

sunflower oil, for pan-frying

coarse sea salt

for the pine kernel sauce

100 g/3½ oz pine kernels

1 garlic clove, peeled

3 tbsp Spanish extra virgin olive oil

1 tbsp lemon juice

3 tbsp water

1 tbsp fresh flat-leaf parsley, chopped

salt and pepper

To make the pine kernel sauce, place the pine kernels and garlic in a food processor or blender and process to form a purée. With the motor still running, gradually add the olive oil, lemon juice and water to form a smooth sauce. Stir in the parsley and season to taste with salt and pepper. Transfer to a serving bowl and reserve until required.

To prepare the courgettes, cut them on the diagonal into thin slices about 5 mm/¼ inch thick. Place the flour and paprika in a polythene bag and mix together. Beat the egg and milk together in a large bowl.

Add the courgette slices to the flour mixture and toss well together until coated. Shake off the excess flour. Heat the sunflower oil in a large, heavy-based frying pan to a depth of about 1 cm/½ inch. Dip the courgette slices, one at a time, into the egg mixture, then slip them into the hot oil. Fry the courgette slices, in batches in a single layer so that they do not overcrowd the frying pan, for 2 minutes, or until they are crisp and golden brown.

Using a slotted spoon, remove the courgette fritters from the frying pan and drain on kitchen paper. Continue until all the courgette slices have been fried.

Serve the courgette fritters piping hot, lightly sprinkled with sea salt, and accompanied by the pine kernel sauce for dipping.

Marinated Aubergines

serves 4

2 aubergines, halved lengthways

4 tbsp Spanish olive oil

2 garlic cloves, finely chopped

2 tbsp fresh parsley, chopped

1 tbsp fresh thyme, chopped

2 tbsp lemon juice

salt and pepper

Make 2–3 slashes in the flesh of the aubergine halves and place, cut-side down, in an ovenproof dish. Season to taste with salt and pepper, pour over the olive oil and sprinkle with the garlic, parsley and thyme. Cover and leave to marinate at room temperature for 2–3 hours.

Preheat the oven to 180°C/350°F/Gas Mark 4. Uncover the dish and roast the aubergines in the preheated oven for 45 minutes. Remove the dish from the oven and turn the aubergines over. Baste with the cooking juices and sprinkle with the lemon juice. Return to the oven and cook for a further 15 minutes.

Transfer the aubergines to serving plates. Spoon over the cooking juices and serve hot or warm.

Aubergine Rolls

serves 4

2 aubergines, sliced thinly
lengthways

5 tbsp olive oil

1 garlic clove, crushed

4 tbsp pesto

175 g/6 oz mozzarella,
grated

basil leaves, torn into
pieces

salt and pepper

fresh basil leaves,
to garnish

Sprinkle the aubergine slices liberally with salt and leave for 10–15 minutes to extract the bitter juices. Turn the slices over and repeat. Rinse well with cold water and drain on kitchen paper.

Heat the olive oil in a large frying pan and add the garlic. Fry the aubergine slices lightly on both sides, a few at a time. Drain them on kitchen paper.

Spread the pesto onto one side of the aubergine slices. Top with the grated mozzarella and sprinkle with the torn basil leaves. Season with a little salt and pepper. Roll up the slices and secure with wooden cocktail sticks.

Arrange the aubergine rolls in a greased ovenproof baking dish. Place in a preheated oven, 180°C/350°F/Gas Mark 4, and bake for 8–10 minutes.

Transfer the aubergine rolls to a warmed serving plate. Scatter with fresh basil leaves and serve at once.

Chillies Rellenos

serves 4–8

3 eggs, separated

55 g/2 oz plain flour

325 g/11½ oz Cheddar or other semi-hard cheese

16 fresh jalapeño chillies

sunflower or corn oil, for deep-frying

Whisk the egg whites in a dry, grease-free bowl until stiff. Beat the egg yolks in a separate bowl, then fold in the whites. Spread out the flour in a shallow dish. Cut 225 g/8 oz of the cheese into 16 sticks and grate the remainder.

Make a slit in the side of each chilli and scrape out the seeds. Rinse the cavities and pat dry with kitchen paper. Place a stick of cheese inside each chilli.

Preheat the grill. Heat the oil for deep-frying to 180–190°C/350–375°F, or until a cube of bread dropped into the oil browns in 30 seconds. Dip the chillies into the egg mixture, then into the flour. Deep-fry, turning occasionally, until golden brown all over. Drain well on kitchen paper.

Arrange the chillies in a flameproof dish and sprinkle over the grated cheese. Place under the grill until the cheese has melted, then serve.

Deep-fried Artichoke Hearts

serves 4–6

60 g/2¼ oz self-raising flour

¼ tsp salt

¼ tsp hot or sweet smoked Spanish paprika

1 garlic clove, crushed

5 tbsp water

1 tbsp olive oil

juice of ½ lemon

12 small globe artichokes

sunflower or Spanish olive oil, for deep-frying

aïoli, to serve

To make the batter, put the flour, salt, paprika and garlic in a large bowl and make a well in the centre. Gradually pour the water and olive oil into the well and mix in the flour mixture from the side, beating constantly, until all the flour is incorporated and a smooth batter forms. Leave to rest while preparing the artichokes.

Fill a bowl with cold water and add the lemon juice. Cut off the stalks of the artichokes. With your hands, break off all the leaves and carefully remove the choke (the mass of silky hairs) by pulling it out with your fingers or scooping it out with a spoon. Immediately put the artichoke hearts in the acidulated water to prevent discoloration.

Cook the artichoke hearts in a saucepan of boiling salted water for 15 minutes, or until tender but still firm, then drain well and pat dry with kitchen paper.

Heat the sunflower or olive oil in a deep-fat fryer to 180–190°C/350–375°F, or until a cube of bread browns in 30 seconds. Spear an artichoke heart on a cocktail stick, dip into the batter and then drop the artichoke heart and cocktail stick into the hot oil. Cook the artichoke hearts, in batches to avoid overcrowding, for 1–2 minutes until golden brown and crisp. Remove with a slotted spoon or draining basket and drain on kitchen paper.

Serve hot, accompanied by a bowl of aïoli for dipping.

2

Meat
Dishes

Sirloin Steak with Sherry

serves 6–8

4 sirloin steaks, about
175–225 g/6–8 oz each
and 2.5 cm/1 inch thick

5 garlic cloves

3 tbsp Spanish olive oil

125 ml/4 fl oz dry Spanish
sherry

salt and pepper

fresh flat-leaf parsley,
chopped, to garnish

crusty bread, to serve

Cut the steaks into 2.5-cm/1-inch cubes and put in a large, shallow dish. Slice 3 of the garlic cloves and set aside. Finely chop the remaining garlic cloves and sprinkle over the steak cubes. Season generously with pepper and mix together well. Cover and leave to marinate in the refrigerator for 1–2 hours.

Heat the oil in a large frying pan, add the garlic slices and cook over a low heat, stirring, for 1 minute, or until golden brown. Increase the heat to medium–high, add the steak cubes and cook, stirring constantly, for 2–3 minutes until browned and almost cooked to your liking.

Add the sherry and cook until it has evaporated slightly. Season to taste with salt and turn into a warmed serving dish. Garnish with chopped parsley and serve hot, accompanied by chunks or slices of crusty bread to mop up the juices.

Beef Skewers with Orange Garlic

serves 6–8

3 tbsp white wine

2 tbsp Spanish olive oil

3 garlic cloves, finely chopped

juice 1 orange

450 g/1 lb rump steak, cubed

450 g/1 lb baby onions, halved

2 orange peppers, deseeded and cut into squares

225 g/8 oz cherry tomatoes, halved

salt and pepper

Mix the wine, olive oil, garlic and orange juice together in a shallow, non-metallic dish. Add the cubes of beef, season to taste with salt and pepper and toss to coat. Cover with clingfilm and leave to marinate in the refrigerator for 2–8 hours.

Preheat the grill to high. Drain the beef, reserving the marinade. Thread the beef, onions, peppers and tomatoes alternately onto several small skewers.

Cook under the hot grill, turning and brushing frequently with the marinade, for 10 minutes, or until cooked through. Transfer to warmed serving plates and serve immediately.

Spanish Meatballs with Cracked Olives

serves 6

55 g/2 oz day-old bread, crusts removed

3 tbsp water

250 g/9 oz lean fresh pork mince

250 g/9 oz lean fresh lamb mince

2 small onions, finely chopped

3 garlic cloves, crushed

1 tsp ground cumin

1 tsp ground coriander

1 egg, lightly beaten

plain flour, for dusting

3 tbsp Spanish olive oil

400 g/14 oz canned chopped tomatoes

5 tbsp dry sherry or red wine

pinch of hot or sweet smoked Spanish paprika

pinch of sugar

175 g/6 oz cracked green Spanish olives in extra virgin olive oil

salt

crusty bread, to serve

Put the bread in a bowl, add the water and leave to soak for 5 minutes. Using your hands, squeeze out as much of the water as possible from the bread and put the bread in a clean bowl. Add the mince, 1 chopped onion, 2 crushed garlic cloves, the cumin, coriander and egg to the bread. Season to taste with salt and, using your hands, mix together well. Dust a plate or baking sheet with flour. Using floured hands, roll the mixture into 30 equal-sized, small balls, put on the plate or baking sheet and roll lightly in the flour.

Heat 2 tablespoons of the oil in a large frying pan, add the meatballs, in batches to avoid overcrowding, and cook over a medium heat, turning frequently, for 8–10 minutes until golden brown on all sides and firm. Remove with a slotted spoon and set aside.

Heat the remaining oil in the frying pan, add the remaining onion and cook, stirring occasionally, for 5 minutes, or until softened but not browned. Add the remaining garlic and cook, stirring, for 30 seconds. Add the tomatoes, sherry, paprika and sugar and season to taste with salt. Bring to the boil, then reduce the heat and simmer for 10 minutes.

Stir the tomato mixture until smooth. Alternatively, turn the tomato mixture into a food processor or blender and process until smooth. Return the sauce to the frying pan.

Carefully return the meatballs to the frying pan, add the olives and simmer for 20 minutes. Serve hot, with crusty bread to mop up the sauce.

Tiny Meatballs in Almond Sauce

serves 6–8

55 g/2 oz white bread, crusts removed

3 tbsp water

450 g/1 lb fresh pork mince

1 large onion, chopped

1 garlic clove, crushed

2 tbsp fresh parsley, chopped, plus extra to garnish

1 egg, beaten

freshly grated nutmeg

plain flour, for coating

2 tbsp Spanish olive oil

lemon juice, to taste

salt and pepper

for the almond sauce

2 tbsp Spanish olive oil

25 g/1 oz white bread

115 g/4 oz blanched almonds

2 garlic cloves, chopped

150 ml/5 fl oz dry white wine

425 ml/15 fl oz vegetable stock

salt and pepper

To prepare the meatballs, place the bread in a bowl, add the water and leave to soak for 5 minutes. With your hands, squeeze out the water and return the bread to a dry bowl. Add the pork, onion, garlic, parsley and egg, then season with grated nutmeg and a little salt and pepper. Knead the ingredients well to form a smooth mixture.

Spread some flour on a plate. With floured hands, shape the meat mixture into about 30 equal-sized balls, then roll each meatball in flour until coated. Heat the olive oil in a large, heavy-based frying pan. Add the meatballs, in batches, and fry for 4–5 minutes, or until browned on all sides. Using a slotted spoon, remove the meatballs from the pan and reserve.

To make the sauce, heat the olive oil in the same frying pan in which the meatballs were fried. Break the bread into pieces, add to the pan with the almonds and fry gently, stirring, until the bread and almonds are golden brown. Add the garlic and fry for a further 30 seconds, then pour in the wine and boil for 1–2 minutes. Season to taste with salt and pepper and leave to cool slightly. Transfer to a food processor or blender. Pour in the vegetable stock and process the mixture until smooth. Return the sauce to the frying pan.

Carefully add the meatballs to the almond sauce and simmer for 25 minutes, or until the meatballs are tender. Taste the sauce and season with salt and pepper if necessary. Transfer to a warmed serving dish, then add a squeeze of lemon juice to taste and sprinkle with chopped parsley. Serve immediately.

Calves' Liver in Almond Saffron Sauce

serves 6

4 tbsp Spanish olive oil

25 g/1 oz white bread

100 g/3½ oz blanched almonds

2 garlic cloves, crushed

pinch of saffron strands

150 ml/5 fl oz dry Spanish sherry or white wine

300 ml/10 fl oz vegetable stock

450 g/1 lb calves' liver

plain flour, for dusting

salt and pepper

fresh flat-leaf parsley, chopped, to garnish

crusty bread, to serve

To make the sauce, heat 2 tablespoons of the oil in a large frying pan. Tear the bread into small pieces and add to the frying pan with the almonds. Cook over a low heat, stirring frequently, for 2 minutes, or until golden brown. Stir in the garlic and cook, stirring, for 30 seconds.

Add the saffron and sherry to the frying pan and season to taste with salt and pepper.

Bring to the boil and continue to boil for 1–2 minutes. Remove from the heat and leave to cool slightly, then transfer the mixture to a food processor. Add the stock and process until smooth. Set aside.

Cut the liver into large bite-sized pieces. Dust lightly with flour and season generously with pepper. Heat the remaining oil in the frying pan, add the liver and cook over a medium heat, stirring constantly, for 2–3 minutes until firm and lightly browned.

Pour the sauce into the frying pan and reheat gently for 1–2 minutes. Transfer to a warmed serving dish and garnish with chopped parsley. Serve hot, accompanied by chunks of crusty bread to mop up the sauce.

Lamb Skewers with Lemon

serves 8

2 garlic cloves, finely chopped

1 Spanish onion, finely chopped

2 tsp finely grated lemon rind

2 tbsp lemon juice

1 tsp fresh thyme leaves

1 tsp ground coriander

1 tsp ground cumin

2 tbsp red wine vinegar

125 ml/4 fl oz Spanish olive oil

1 kg/2 lb 4 oz lamb fillet, cut into 2-cm/¾-inch pieces

lemon slices, to garnish

Mix the garlic, onion, lemon rind, lemon juice, thyme, coriander, cumin, vinegar and olive oil together in a large, shallow, non-metallic dish, whisking well until thoroughly combined.

Thread the pieces of lamb onto 16 wooden skewers and add to the dish, turning well to coat. Cover with clingfilm and leave to marinate in the refrigerator for 2–8 hours, turning occasionally.

Preheat the grill to medium. Drain the skewers, reserving the marinade. Cook under the hot grill, turning frequently and brushing with the marinade, for 10 minutes, or until tender and cooked to your liking.

Serve immediately, garnished with lemon slices.

Spare Ribs Coated in Paprika Sauce

serves 6

Spanish olive oil, for oiling

1.25 kg/2 lb 12 oz pork spare ribs

100 ml/3½ fl oz dry Spanish sherry

5 tsp hot or sweet smoked Spanish paprika

2 garlic cloves, crushed

1 tbsp dried oregano

150 ml/5 fl oz water

salt

Preheat the oven to 220°C/425°F/Gas Mark 7. Oil a large roasting tin. If the butcher has not already done so, cut the sheets of spare ribs into individual ribs. If possible, cut each spare rib in half widthways. Put the spare ribs in the prepared tin, in a single layer, and roast in the preheated oven for 20 minutes.

Meanwhile, make the sauce. Put the sherry, paprika, garlic, oregano, water and salt to taste in a jug and mix together well.

Reduce the oven temperature to 180°C/350°F/Gas Mark 4. Pour off the fat from the tin, then pour the sauce over the spare ribs and turn the spare ribs to coat on both sides. Roast for a further 45 minutes, until tender, basting the spare ribs with the sauce once halfway through the cooking time.

Pile the spare ribs into a warmed serving dish. Bring the sauce in the roasting tin to the boil on the hob, then reduce the heat and simmer until reduced by half. Pour the sauce over the spare ribs and serve hot.

Miniature Pork Brochettes

makes 12

450 g/1 lb lean boneless pork

3 tbsp extra virgin olive oil, plus extra for oiling (optional)

grated rind and juice of 1 large lemon

2 garlic cloves, crushed

2 tbsp fresh flat-leaf parsley, chopped, plus extra to garnish

1 tbsp ras-el-hanout spice blend

salt and pepper

Cut the pork into pieces about 2 cm/3/4 inch square and put in a large, shallow, non-metallic dish that will hold the pieces in a single layer.

To prepare the marinade, put all the remaining ingredients in a bowl and mix well together. Pour the marinade over the pork and toss the meat in it until well coated. Cover the dish and leave to marinate in the refrigerator for 8 hours or overnight, stirring the pork 2–3 times.

Preheat the grill to medium–high. Thread about 3 marinated pork pieces, leaving a little space between each piece, onto a skewer. Cook the brochettes for 10–15 minutes or until tender and lightly charred, turning several times and basting with the remaining marinade during cooking. Serve the pork brochettes piping hot, garnished with parsley.

Serrano Ham Croquettes

serves 4

4 tbsp Spanish olive oil

1 small onion, finely chopped

1 garlic clove, crushed

4 tbsp plain flour

200 ml/7 fl oz milk

200 g/7 oz Serrano ham or cooked ham, in one piece, finely diced

pinch of hot or sweet smoked Spanish paprika

1 egg

55 g/2 oz day-old white breadcrumbs

sunflower oil, for deep-frying

salt

aïoli, to serve

Heat the olive oil in a saucepan, add the onion and cook over a medium heat, stirring occasionally, for 5 minutes, or until softened but not browned. Add the garlic and cook, stirring, for 30 seconds. Stir in the flour and cook over a low heat, stirring constantly, for 1 minute without the mixture colouring. Remove the saucepan from the heat and gradually stir in the milk to form a smooth sauce. Return to the heat and slowly bring to the boil, stirring constantly, until the sauce boils and thickens.

Remove the saucepan from the heat, stir in the ham and paprika and season to taste with salt. Spread the mixture in a shallow dish and leave to cool, then cover and chill in the refrigerator for at least 2 hours or overnight.

When the mixture has chilled, break the egg onto a plate and beat lightly. Spread the breadcrumbs on a separate plate. Using wet hands, form the ham mixture into 8 even-sized pieces and form each piece into a cylindrical shape. Dip the croquettes, one at a time, into the beaten egg, then roll in the breadcrumbs to coat. Put on a plate and chill in the refrigerator for at least 1 hour.

Heat enough sunflower oil for deep-frying in a deep-fat fryer to 180–190°C/350–375°F, or until a cube of bread browns in 30 seconds. Add the croquettes, in batches to avoid overcrowding, and cook for 5 minutes, or until golden brown and crisp. Remove and drain on kitchen paper. Keep hot in a warm oven while you cook the remaining croquettes. Serve hot with aïoli.

Empanadillas with Ham & Goat's Cheese

serves 16

1 tbsp Spanish olive oil

1 small onion, finely chopped

1 garlic clove, crushed

150 g/5½ oz soft goat's cheese

175 g/6 oz thickly sliced cooked ham, finely chopped

50 g/1¾ oz capers, chopped

½ tsp hot or sweet smoked Spanish paprika

500 g/1 lb 2 oz ready-made puff pastry, thawed if frozen

plain flour, for dusting

beaten egg, for glazing

salt

Preheat the oven to 200°C/400°F/Gas Mark 6. Dampen several large baking sheets. Heat the oil in a large frying pan, add the onion and cook over a medium heat, stirring occasionally, for 5 minutes, or until softened but not browned. Add the garlic and cook, stirring, for 30 seconds. Put the goat's cheese in a bowl, add the ham, capers, onion mixture and paprika and mix together well. Season to taste with salt.

Thinly roll out the pastry on a lightly floured work surface. Using a plain, 8-cm/3¼-inch round cutter, cut out 32 rounds, re-rolling the trimmings as necessary. Using a teaspoon, put an equal, small amount of the goat's cheese mixture in the centre of each pastry round. Dampen the edges of the pastry with a little water and fold one half over the other to form a crescent and enclose the filling. Pinch the edges together with your fingers to seal, then press with the tines of a fork to seal further. Transfer to the prepared baking sheets.

With the tip of a sharp knife, make a small slit in the top of each pastry and brush with beaten egg to glaze. Bake in the preheated oven for 15 minutes, or until risen and golden brown. Serve warm.

Mushrooms Stuffed with Spinach & Bacon

serves 4

225 g/8 oz fresh baby spinach leaves

4 portobello mushrooms

3 tbsp olive oil

55 g/2 oz rindless bacon, finely diced

2 garlic cloves, crushed

55 g/2 oz fresh white or brown breadcrumbs

2 tbsp fresh basil, chopped

salt and pepper

Preheat the oven to 200°C/400°F/Gas Mark 6. Rinse the spinach and place in a saucepan with only the water clinging to the leaves. Cook for 2–3 minutes, until wilted. Drain, squeezing out as much liquid as possible, and chop finely.

Cut the stalks from the mushrooms and chop finely, reserving the whole caps.

Heat 2 tablespoons of the oil in a frying pan. Add the mushroom caps, rounded-side down, and fry for 1 minute. Remove from the frying pan and arrange, rounded-side down, in a large baking dish.

Add the chopped mushroom stalks, bacon and garlic to the frying pan and fry for 5 minutes. Stir in the spinach, breadcrumbs, basil and salt and pepper to taste. Mix well and divide the stuffing between the mushroom caps.

Drizzle the remaining oil over the top and bake in the oven for 20 minutes, until crisp and golden.

Chorizo in Red Wine

serves 6

200 g/7 oz chorizo sausage

200 ml/7 fl oz Spanish red wine

2 tbsp brandy (optional)

fresh flat-leaf parsley, chopped, to garnish

crusty bread, to serve

Using a fork, prick the chorizo in 3 or 4 places. Place the chorizo and wine in a large saucepan. Bring the wine to the boil, then reduce the heat, cover and simmer gently for 15–20 minutes. Transfer the chorizo and wine to a bowl or dish, cover and leave the sausage to marinate in the wine for 8 hours or overnight.

Remove the chorizo from the bowl or dish and reserve the wine. Remove the outer casing from the chorizo and cut the sausage into 5-mm/$\frac{1}{4}$-inch slices. Place the slices in a large, heavy-based frying pan or flameproof serving dish.

If you are adding the brandy, pour it into a small saucepan and heat gently. Pour the brandy over the chorizo slices, stand well back and set alight. When the flames have died down, shake the pan gently, add the reserved wine to the saucepan and cook over a high heat until almost all of the wine has evaporated.

Serve the chorizo in red wine piping hot, in the pan or dish in which it was cooked, sprinkled with parsley to garnish. Accompany with chunks or slices of bread to mop up the juices and provide wooden cocktail sticks to spear the pieces of chorizo.

Chickpeas & Chorizo

serves 4–6

250 g/9 oz chorizo sausage in 1 piece, outer casing removed

4 tbsp Spanish olive oil

1 onion, finely chopped

1 large garlic clove, crushed

400 g/14 oz canned chickpeas, drained and rinsed

6 pimientos del piquillo, drained, patted dry and sliced

1 tbsp sherry vinegar, or to taste

salt and pepper

fresh parsley, chopped, to garnish

crusty bread slices, to serve

Cut the chorizo into 1-cm/½-inch dice. Heat the oil in a large, heavy-based frying pan over a medium heat. Add the onion and garlic and fry, stirring occasionally, until the onion is softened but not browned. Stir in the chorizo and fry until heated through.

Transfer the mixture to a bowl and stir in the chickpeas and pimientos. Splash with sherry vinegar and season to taste with salt and pepper. Serve hot or at room temperature, generously sprinkled with parsley, with plenty of crusty bread.

Spicy Fried Bread & Chorizo

serves 6–8

200 g/7 oz chorizo sausage, outer casing removed

4 thick slices 2-day-old country bread

Spanish olive oil, for pan-frying

3 garlic cloves, finely chopped

fresh parsley sprigs and paprika, to garnish

Cut the chorizo into 1-cm/½-inch thick slices and cut the bread, with its crusts still on, into 1-cm/½-inch cubes.

Add enough olive oil to a large, heavy-based frying pan to generously cover the base. Heat the oil, add the garlic and fry for 30 seconds–1 minute, or until lightly browned.

Add the bread cubes to the pan and fry, stirring constantly, until golden brown and crisp. Add the chorizo slices and fry for 1–2 minutes, or until hot. Using a slotted spoon, remove the bread cubes and chorizo from the frying pan and drain well on kitchen paper.

Turn the fried bread and chorizo into a warmed serving bowl and toss together. Garnish the dish with parsley sprigs and a sprinkling of paprika and serve warm. Accompany with wooden cocktail sticks so that a piece of sausage and a cube of bread can be speared together for eating.

Chorizo & Mushroom Kebabs

serves 8

2 tbsp Spanish olive oil

24 slices chorizo sausage, each about 1 cm/½ inch thick (about 100 g/3½ oz)

24 button mushrooms, wiped

1 green pepper, grilled, peeled and cut into 24 squares

Heat the olive oil in a frying pan over a medium heat. Add the chorizo and fry for 20 seconds, stirring.

Add the mushrooms and continue frying for a further 1–2 minutes until the mushrooms begin to brown and absorb the fat in the frying pan.

Thread a green pepper square, a piece of chorizo and a mushroom onto a wooden cocktail stick. Continue until all the ingredients are used. Serve hot or at room temperature.

ken in Lemon &

...ge skinless, boneless chicken breasts

5 tbsp extra virgin olive oil

1 onion, finely chopped

6 garlic cloves, finely chopped

grated rind of 1 lemon, finely pared rind of 1 lemon and juice of both lemons

4 tbsp chopped fresh flat-leaf parsley

salt and pepper

lemon wedges and crusty bread, to serve

Using a sharp knife, slice the chicken breasts widthways into very thin slices. Heat the olive oil in a large, heavy-based frying pan, add the onion and fry for 5 minutes, or until softened but not browned. Add the garlic and fry for a further 30 seconds.

Add the sliced chicken to the pan and fry gently for 5–10 minutes, stirring from time to time, until all the ingredients are lightly browned and the chicken is tender.

Add the grated lemon rind and the lemon juice and let it bubble. At the same time, deglaze the pan by scraping and stirring all the bits on the base of the pan into the juices with a wooden spoon. Remove the pan from the heat, stir in the parsley and season to taste with salt and pepper.

Transfer the chicken in lemon and garlic to a warmed serving dish. Sprinkle with the pared lemon rind, and serve, piping hot, with lemon wedges for squeezing over the chicken, accompanied by chunks or slices of crusty bread for mopping up the lemon and garlic juices.

Chicken Morsels Fried in Batter

serves 6–8

500 g/1 lb 2 oz skinless, boneless chicken thighs

3 tbsp olive oil

juice of ½ lemon

2 garlic cloves, crushed

8 tbsp flour

vegetable oil for deep-frying

2 eggs, beaten

salt and pepper

coarsely chopped fresh flat-leaf parsley, to garnish

lemon wedges, to serve

Cut the chicken thighs into 4-cm/1½-inch chunks. Mix the olive oil, lemon juice, garlic, salt and pepper in a bowl. Add the chicken pieces and leave to marinate at room temperature for an hour, or overnight in the fridge.

Spread the flour on a plate and mix with a pinch of salt and plenty of pepper.

When ready to cook, remove the chicken pieces from the marinade and drain.

Heat the vegetable oil in a deep-fat fryer or large saucepan to 180–190°C/350–375°F, or until a cube of bread browns in 30 seconds. Roll the chicken in the seasoned flour and then in beaten egg. Immediately drop into the hot oil, a few pieces at a time, and deep-fry for about 5 minutes, until golden and crisp, turning occasionally with tongs. Drain on crumpled kitchen paper.

Place the chicken pieces in a warm serving dish and sprinkle with parsley. Serve hot with thick wedges of lemon.

Sautéed Chicken with Crispy Garlic Slices

serves 8

8 skin-on chicken thighs, boned if available

hot or sweet smoked Spanish paprika, to taste

4 tbsp Spanish olive oil

10 garlic cloves, sliced

125 ml/4 fl oz dry white wine

1 bay leaf

salt

fresh parsley, chopped, to garnish

crusty bread, to serve (optional)

If necessary, halve the chicken thighs and remove the bones, then cut the flesh into bite-sized pieces, leaving the skin on. Season with paprika.

Heat the oil in a large frying pan or a flameproof casserole, add the garlic slices and cook over a medium heat, stirring frequently, for 1 minute until golden brown. Remove with a slotted spoon and drain on kitchen paper.

Add the chicken thighs to the pan and cook, turning occasionally, for 10 minutes, or until tender and golden brown on all sides. Add the wine and bay leaf and bring to the boil. Reduce the heat and simmer, stirring occasionally, for 10 minutes, or until most of the liquid has evaporated and the juices run clear when a skewer is inserted into the thickest part of the meat. Season to taste with salt.

Transfer the chicken to a warmed serving dish and sprinkle over the reserved garlic slices. Scatter with chopped parsley to garnish and serve with chunks of crusty bread to mop up the juices, if desired.

Chicken Rolls with Olives

serves 6–8

115 g/4 oz black Spanish olives in oil, drained and 2 tbsp oil reserved

140 g/5 oz butter, softened

4 tbsp fresh parsley, chopped

4 skinless, boneless chicken breasts

Preheat the oven to 200°C/400°F/Gas Mark 6. Stone and finely chop the olives. Mix the olives, butter and parsley together in a bowl.

Place the chicken breasts between 2 sheets of clingfilm and beat gently with a meat mallet or the side of a rolling pin.

Spread the olive and herb butter over one side of each flattened chicken breast and roll up. Secure with a wooden cocktail stick or tie with clean string if necessary.

Place the chicken rolls in an ovenproof dish. Drizzle over the oil from the olive jar and bake in the preheated oven for 45–55 minutes, or until tender and the juices run clear when the chicken is pierced with the point of a sharp knife.

Transfer the chicken rolls to a chopping board and discard the cocktail sticks or string. Using a sharp knife, cut into slices, then transfer to warmed serving plates and serve.

Chicken Wings with Tomato Dressing

serves 6–8

175 ml/6 fl oz Spanish olive oil

3 garlic cloves, finely chopped

1 tsp ground cumin

1 kg/2 lb 4 oz chicken wings

2 tomatoes, peeled, deseeded and diced

5 tbsp white wine vinegar

1 tbsp shredded fresh basil leaves

Preheat the oven to 180°C/350°F/Gas Mark 4. Mix 1 tablespoon of the oil with the garlic and cumin in a shallow dish. Cut off and discard the tips of the chicken wings and add the wings to the spice mixture, turning to coat. Cover with clingfilm and leave to marinate in a cool place for 15 minutes.

Heat 3 tablespoons of the remaining oil in a large, heavy-based frying pan. Add the chicken wings, in batches, and cook, turning frequently, until golden brown. Transfer to a roasting tin.

Roast the chicken wings for 10–15 minutes, or until tender and the juices run clear when the point of a sharp knife is inserted into the thickest part of the meat.

Meanwhile, mix the remaining olive oil, the tomatoes, vinegar and basil together in a bowl.

Using tongs, transfer the chicken wings to a non-metallic dish. Pour the dressing over them, turning to coat. Cover with clingfilm, leave to cool, then chill for 4 hours. Remove from the refrigerator 30–60 minutes before serving to return them to room temperature.

Chicken Salad with Raisins & Pine Kernels

serves 6–8

50 ml/2 fl oz red wine vinegar

25 g/1 oz caster sugar

1 bay leaf

pared rind of 1 lemon

150 g/5½ oz seedless raisins

4 large skinless, boneless chicken breasts, about 600 g/1 lb 5 oz in total

5 tbsp Spanish olive oil

1 garlic clove, finely chopped

150 g/5½ oz pine kernels

100 ml/3½ fl oz Spanish extra virgin olive oil

1 small bunch fresh flat-leaf parsley, finely chopped

salt and pepper

To make the dressing, put the vinegar, sugar, bay leaf and lemon rind in a saucepan and bring to the boil, then remove from the heat. Stir in the raisins and leave to cool.

When the dressing is cool, slice the chicken breasts widthways into very thin slices. Heat the olive oil in a large frying pan, add the chicken slices and cook over a medium heat, stirring occasionally, for 8–10 minutes until lightly browned and tender.

Add the garlic and pine kernels and cook, stirring constantly and shaking the pan, for 1 minute, or until the pine kernels are golden brown. Season to taste with salt and pepper.

Pour the cooled dressing into a large bowl, discarding the bay leaf and lemon rind. Add the extra virgin olive oil and whisk together. Season to taste with salt and pepper. Add the chicken mixture and parsley and toss together. Turn the salad into a serving dish and serve warm or, if serving cold, cover and chill in the refrigerator for 2–3 hours before serving.

Fish &
Seafood
Dishes

Salt Cod Fritters

serves 16

250 g/9 oz pre-soaked salt cod in 1 piece

140 g/5 oz plain flour

1 tsp baking powder

¼ tsp salt

1 large egg, lightly beaten

about 150 ml/5 fl oz milk

2 lemon slices

2 fresh parsley sprigs

1 bay leaf

½ tbsp garlic-flavoured olive oil

85 g/3 oz fresh baby spinach, rinsed

¼ tsp smoked sweet, mild or hot Spanish paprika, to taste

Spanish olive oil, for frying

coarse sea salt (optional)

aïoli, to serve

To make the batter, sift the flour, baking powder and salt into a large bowl and make a well. Mix the egg with 100 ml/3½ fl oz of the milk and pour into the well in the flour, stirring to make a smooth batter with a thick coating consistency. If it seems too thick, gradually stir in the remaining milk, then leave to stand for at least 1 hour.

Transfer the salt cod to a large frying pan over a medium heat. Add the lemon slices, parsley sprigs, bay leaf and enough water to cover and bring to the boil. Reduce the heat and simmer for 30–45 minutes until the fish is tender and flakes easily.

Meanwhile, prepare the spinach. Heat the garlic-flavoured olive oil in a small saucepan over a medium heat. Add the spinach with just the water clinging to the leaves and cook for 3–4 minutes until wilted. Drain the spinach in a sieve, using the back of a spoon to press out any excess moisture. Finely chop the spinach, then stir it into the batter with the paprika.

Remove the fish from the water and flake the flesh into pieces, removing all the skin and tiny bones. Stir the flesh into the batter.

Heat 5 cm/2 inch of olive oil in a heavy-based frying pan to 180–190°C/350–375°F, or until a cube of bread browns in 30 seconds. Use a greased tablespoon or measuring spoon to drop spoonfuls of the batter into the oil and fry for 8–10 minutes until golden brown. Work in batches to avoid crowding the pan. Use a slotted spoon to transfer the fritters to kitchen paper to drain and sprinkle with sea salt, if using. Serve hot or at room temperature with aïoli for dipping.

Monkfish, Rosemary & Bacon Skewers

serves 6

250 g/9 oz monkfish fillet

12 fresh rosemary stems

3 tbsp Spanish olive oil

juice of ½ small lemon

1 garlic clove, crushed

6 rindless thick back bacon rashers

salt and pepper

lemon wedges, to garnish

aïoli, to serve

Slice the fillet in half lengthways, then cut each half into 12 bite-sized chunks to give a total of 24 pieces. Put the monkfish pieces in a large bowl. To prepare the rosemary skewers, strip the leaves off the stems and reserve them, leaving a few leaves at one end.

For the marinade, finely chop the reserved leaves and whisk with the oil, lemon juice, garlic and salt and pepper to taste in a non-metallic bowl. Add the monkfish pieces and toss until coated in the marinade. Cover and leave to marinate in the refrigerator for 1–2 hours.

Cut each bacon rasher in half lengthways, then in half widthways, and roll up each piece. Thread 2 monkfish pieces alternately with 2 bacon rolls onto the prepared rosemary skewers.

Preheat the grill. Cook the skewers, turning frequently and basting with any remaining marinade, for 10 minutes, or until cooked. Serve hot, garnished with lemon wedges for squeezing over and accompanied by a bowl of aïoli for dipping.

Tuna with Pimiento-stuffed Olives

serves 6

2 fresh tuna steaks, weighing about 250 g/ 9 oz in total and about 2.5 cm/1 inch thick

5 tbsp of extra virgin olive oil

3 tbsp red wine vinegar

4 sprigs of fresh thyme, plus extra to garnish

1 bay leaf

2 tbsp plain flour

1 onion, finely chopped

2 garlic cloves, finely chopped

85 g/3 oz pimiento-stuffed green olives, halved

salt and pepper

Remove the skin from the tuna steaks, then cut the steaks in half along the grain of the fish. Cut each half into 1-cm/1/2-inch thick slices against the grain.

Put 3 tablespoons of the olive oil and the vinegar in a large, shallow, non-metallic dish. Strip the leaves from the sprigs of thyme and add these to the dish with the bay leaf and salt and pepper to taste. Add the prepared strips of tuna, cover the dish and leave to marinate in the refrigerator for 8 hours or overnight.

The next day, put the flour in a polythene bag. Remove the tuna strips from the marinade, reserving the marinade for later, add them to the bag of flour and toss well until they are lightly coated.

Heat the remaining olive oil in a large, heavy-based frying pan. Add the onion and garlic and gently fry for 5–10 minutes, or until softened and golden brown. Add the tuna strips to the pan and fry for 2–5 minutes, turning several times, until the fish becomes opaque. Add the reserved marinade and olives to the pan and cook for a further 1–2 minutes, stirring, until the fish is tender and the sauce has thickened.

Serve the tuna and olives piping hot, garnished with thyme sprigs.

Sardines with Romesco Sauce

serves 6

24 fresh sardines, scaled, cleaned and heads removed

115 g/4 oz plain flour

4 eggs, lightly beaten

250 g/9 oz fresh white breadcrumbs

85 g/3 oz fresh mixed herbs, chopped

vegetable oil, for deep-frying

for the romesco sauce

1 red pepper, halved and deseeded

2 tomatoes, halved

4 garlic cloves

125 ml/4 fl oz Spanish olive oil

1 slice white bread, diced

4 tbsp blanched almonds

1 fresh red chilli, deseeded and chopped

2 shallots, chopped

1 tsp paprika

2 tbsp red wine vinegar

2 tsp sugar

First make the sauce. Preheat the oven to 220°C/425°F/ Gas Mark 7. Place the pepper, tomatoes and garlic in an ovenproof dish and drizzle over 1 tablespoon of the olive oil, turning to coat. Bake in the preheated oven for 20–25 minutes, then remove from the oven and cool. Peel off the skins and place the flesh in a food processor.

Heat 1 tablespoon of the remaining oil in a frying pan. Add the bread and almonds and cook over a low heat for a few minutes, or until browned. Remove and drain on kitchen paper. Add the chilli, shallots and paprika to the pan and cook for a further 5 minutes, or until the shallots are softened.

Transfer the almond mixture and shallot mixture to a food processor and add a splash of water. Process to a paste. With the motor still running, gradually add the remaining oil through the feeder tube. Transfer to a bowl, cover and reserve.

Place the sardines, skin-side up, on a chopping board and press along the length of the spines with your thumbs. Turn over and remove and discard the bones. Place the flour and eggs in separate bowls. Mix the breadcrumbs and herbs together in a third bowl. Toss the fish in the flour, the eggs, then in the breadcrumbs.

Heat the vegetable oil in a large saucepan to 180–190°C/ 350–375°F, or until a cube of bread browns in 30 seconds. Deep-fry the fish for 4–5 minutes, or until golden and tender. Drain and serve with the sauce.

Deep-fried Whitebait

serves 4

450 g/1 lb fresh whitebait

100 g/3½ oz plain flour

50 g/1¾ oz cornflour

½ tsp salt

200 ml/7 fl oz cold water

1 egg

a few ice cubes

vegetable oil, for frying

for the chilli mayonnaise

1 fresh red chilli

1 egg yolk

1 tbsp lime juice

2 tbsp chopped fresh coriander

200 ml/7 fl oz olive oil

salt and pepper

For the mayonnaise, deseed and finely chop the chilli. Place the egg yolk, lime juice, chilli, coriander and seasoning in a food processor and process until foaming. With the machine still running, gradually add the olive oil, drop by drop, until the mixture begins to thicken. Continue adding the oil in a steady stream until all the oil has been incorporated. Taste and adjust the seasoning and add a little hot water if the mixture is too thick. Reserve.

For the whitebait, rinse the fish and pat dry. Reserve on kitchen paper. Sift together the plain flour, cornflour and salt into a large bowl. Whisk together the water, egg and ice cubes, then pour onto the flour mix. Whisk briefly until the mixture is runny, but still lumpy with dry bits of flour still apparent.

Meanwhile, fill a deep saucepan about a third full with vegetable oil and heat to 190°C/375°F, or until a cube of bread browns in 30 seconds.

Dip the whitebait, a few at a time, into the batter and carefully drop into the hot oil. Deep-fry for 1 minute until the batter is crisp but not browned. Drain on kitchen paper and keep warm while you cook the remaining fish. Serve hot with the mayonnaise.

Mixed Seafood Kebabs with Chilli & Lime Glaze

serves 4

16 raw tiger prawns, deveined and shelled but with tails intact

350 g/12 oz monkfish or hake fillet

350 g/12 oz salmon fillet, skinned

2.5-cm/1-inch piece fresh ginger

4 tbsp sweet chilli sauce

grated rind and juice of 1 lime

sunflower or Spanish olive oil, for oiling (optional)

lime wedges, to serve

Rinse the prawns under cold running water and pat dry with kitchen paper. Cut the monkfish and salmon into 2.5-cm/1-inch pieces.

Grate the ginger into a sieve set over a large, non-metallic bowl to catch the juice. Squeeze the grated ginger to extract all the juice and discard the pulp.

Add the chilli sauce and lime rind and juice to the ginger juice and mix together. Add the prepared seafood and stir to coat in the marinade. Cover and leave to marinate in the refrigerator for 30 minutes.

Meanwhile, if using wooden skewers, soak 8 in cold water for about 30 minutes to help prevent them from burning and the food sticking to them during cooking. If using metal skewers, lightly brush with oil.

Preheat the grill to high and line the grill pan with foil. Remove the seafood from the marinade, reserving the remaining marinade, and thread an equal quantity onto each prepared skewer, leaving a little space between each piece. Arrange in the grill pan. Cook the skewers under the grill, turning once and brushing with the reserved marinade, for 6–8 minutes until cooked through. Serve hot, drizzled with the marinade in the grill pan and with lime wedges for squeezing over.

Batter-fried Fish Sticks

serves 6

115 g/4 oz plain flour, plus extra for dusting

pinch of salt

1 egg, beaten

1 tbsp Spanish olive oil

150 ml/5 fl oz water

600 g/1 lb 5 oz firm-fleshed white fish fillet, such as monkfish or hake

sunflower or Spanish olive oil, for deep-frying

lemon wedges, to serve

To make the batter, put the flour and salt into a large bowl and make a well in the centre. Pour the egg and olive oil into the well, then gradually add the water, mixing in the flour from the side and beating constantly, until all the flour is incorporated and a smooth batter forms.

Cut the fish into sticks about 2 cm/³⁄₄ inch wide and 5 cm/2 inches long. Dust lightly with flour so that the batter sticks to them when they are dipped in it.

Heat enough sunflower or olive oil for deep-frying in a deep-fat fryer to 180–190°C/350–375°F, or until a cube of bread browns in 30 seconds. Spear a fish stick onto a cocktail stick, dip into the batter and then drop the fish and cocktail stick into the hot oil. Cook the fish sticks, in batches to avoid overcrowding, for 5 minutes, or until golden brown. Remove with a slotted spoon or draining basket and drain on kitchen paper. Keep hot in a warm oven while cooking the remaining fish sticks. Serve the fish sticks hot, with lemon wedges for squeezing over.

Roman Dip with Anchovy Rounds

serves 12

1 egg

150 g/5½ oz stoned black Spanish olives

50 g/1¾ oz canned anchovy fillets in olive oil, drained and oil reserved

2 garlic cloves, 1 crushed and 1 peeled but kept whole

1 tbsp capers

½ tsp hot or sweet smoked Spanish paprika

1 tbsp Spanish brandy or sherry

4 tbsp Spanish extra virgin olive oil

1 small baguette

pepper

Put the egg in a saucepan, cover with cold water and slowly bring to the boil. Reduce the heat and simmer gently for 10 minutes. Immediately drain the egg and rinse under cold running water to cool. Gently tap the egg to crack the shell and leave until cold.

When the egg is cold, crack the shell all over and remove it. Put the egg in a food processor and add the olives, 2 of the anchovy fillets, the crushed garlic, capers, paprika and brandy and process to a rough paste. With the motor running, very slowly add 1 tablespoon of the reserved oil from the anchovies and the extra virgin olive oil in a thin, steady stream. Season the dip to taste with pepper.

Turn the dip into a small serving bowl, cover and chill in the refrigerator until ready to serve.

To make the anchovy rounds, put the remaining anchovy fillets, remaining reserved oil from the anchovies and garlic clove in a mortar and, using a pestle, pound together to a paste. Turn the paste into a bowl, cover and chill in the refrigerator until ready to serve.

When ready to serve, preheat the grill to high. Slice the baguette into 2.5-cm/1-inch rounds and toast under the grill until golden brown on both sides. Spread the anchovy paste very thinly on the toasted bread rounds and serve with the dip.

Empanadillas with Tuna & Olives

serves 16

175 g/6 oz canned tuna in olive oil

1 small onion, finely chopped

1 garlic clove, finely chopped

50 g/1¾ oz pimiento-stuffed Spanish olives, finely chopped

25 g/1 oz pine kernels

500 g/1 lb 2 oz ready-made puff pastry, thawed if frozen

salt and pepper

plain flour, for dusting

beaten egg, for glazing

Drain the tuna, reserving the oil, put in a large bowl and set aside. Heat 1 tablespoon of the reserved oil from the tuna in a large frying pan, add the onion and cook over a medium heat, stirring occasionally, for 5 minutes, or until softened but not browned. Add the garlic and cook, stirring, for 30 seconds until softened.

Mash the tuna with a fork, then add the onion mixture, olives and pine kernels and mix together well. Season to taste with salt and pepper.

Preheat the oven to 200°C/400°F/Gas Mark 6. Dampen several large baking sheets. Thinly roll out the pastry on a lightly floured work surface. Using a plain, 8-cm/3¼-inch round cutter, cut out 32 rounds, re-rolling the trimmings as necessary. Using a teaspoon, put an equal, small amount of the tuna mixture in the centre of each pastry round.

Dampen the edges of the pastry with a little water and fold one half over the other to form a crescent and enclose the filling. Pinch the edges together with your fingers to seal, then press with the tines of a fork to seal further. Transfer to the prepared baking sheets.

With the tip of a sharp knife, make a small slit in the top of each pastry and brush with beaten egg to glaze. Bake in the preheated oven for 15 minutes, or until risen and golden brown. Serve warm.

Prawn & Haricot Toasties

serves 4

3 garlic cloves

4 tbsp Spanish olive oil

1 Spanish onion, halved and finely chopped

400 g/14 oz canned haricot beans, drained and rinsed

4 tomatoes, diced

4 thick slices country bread

280 g/10 oz cooked peeled prawns

salt and pepper

watercress, to garnish

Halve 1 of the garlic cloves and reserve. Finely chop the remaining cloves. Heat 2 tablespoons of the olive oil in a large, heavy-based frying pan. Add the chopped garlic and onion and cook over a low heat, stirring occasionally, for 5 minutes, or until softened.

Stir in the beans and tomatoes and season to taste with salt and pepper. Cook gently for a further 5 minutes.

Meanwhile, toast the bread on both sides, then rub each slice with the cut sides of the reserved garlic and drizzle with the remaining oil.

Stir the prawns into the bean mixture and heat through gently for 2–3 minutes. Pile the bean and prawn mixture onto the toasts and serve immediately, garnished with watercress.

Pan-fried Prawns

serves 4

4 garlic cloves

20–24 unshelled large raw prawns

125 g/4½ oz butter

4 tbsp olive oil

6 tbsp brandy

salt and pepper

2 tbsp fresh parsley, chopped, to garnish

lemon wedges, to serve

Using a sharp knife, peel and slice the garlic.

Wash the prawns and pat dry using kitchen paper.

Melt the butter with the oil in a large frying pan, add the garlic and prawns, and fry over a high heat, stirring, for 3–4 minutes, until the prawns are pink.

Sprinkle with brandy and season with salt and pepper to taste. Sprinkle with parsley and serve immediately, with lemon wedges for squeezing over them.

Calamares

serves 6

450 g/1 lb prepared squid

plain flour, for coating

sunflower oil, for deep-frying

salt

lemon wedges, to serve

aïoli, to serve

Slice the squid into 1-cm/½-inch rings and halve the tentacles if large. Rinse and dry well on kitchen paper so that they do not spit during cooking. Dust the squid rings with flour so that they are lightly coated.

Heat the sunflower oil in a deep fryer to 180–190°C/ 350–375°F, or until a cube of bread browns in 30 seconds. Carefully add the squid rings, in batches so that the temperature of the oil does not drop, and fry for 2–3 minutes, or until golden brown and crisp all over, turning several times. Do not overcook as the squid will become tough and rubbery rather than moist and tender.

Using a slotted spoon, remove the fried squid from the deep fryer and drain well on kitchen paper. Keep hot in a warm oven while you fry the remaining squid rings.

Sprinkle the fried squid rings with salt and serve piping hot, with lemon wedges for squeezing over them, and a bowl of aïoli, for dipping.

Seared Squid & Golden Potatoes

serves 8

1 kg/2 lb 4 oz new potatoes

6 tbsp Spanish olive oil

1 large onion, thinly sliced

2 garlic cloves, finely chopped

1 kg/2 lb 4 oz cleaned squid bodies, thinly sliced

6 tbsp dry white wine

1 small bunch fresh flat-leaf parsley, finely chopped

salt and pepper

lemon wedges, to serve

Put the potatoes in a saucepan of water and bring to the boil. Reduce the heat and simmer for 20 minutes, or until tender. Drain well.

Heat 4 tablespoons of oil in a large flameproof casserole, add the potatoes and cook over a medium heat, stirring occasionally, for 10 minutes, or until beginning to turn brown. Add the onion and cook, stirring occasionally, for 10 minutes until golden brown. Add the garlic and cook, stirring, for 30 seconds until softened. Push all the ingredients to the side of the casserole.

If necessary, add the remaining oil to the casserole. Add the squid slices and cook over a high heat, stirring occasionally, for 2 minutes, or until golden brown. Add the wine and cook for a further 1–2 minutes. Add most of the parsley, reserving a little to garnish, and mix the potatoes, onions and garlic with the squid. Season to taste with salt and pepper.

Serve hot, in the casserole, sprinkled with the reserved parsley to garnish and with lemon wedges for squeezing over.

Scallop Tartlets with Pea & Mint Purée

makes 12

100 g/4 oz puff pastry rolled to a depth of 3 mm/⅛ inch

4 large fresh scallops, cleaned and roe removed

extra virgin olive oil, for coating the scallops

salt and pepper

for the pea & mint purée

50 g/2 oz cooked peas

small clove garlic, grated

1 tbsp extra virgin olive oil

1 tbsp mint, chopped

1 tbsp soured cream

1 tsp lemon juice

salt and pepper

Preheat the oven to 180°C/ 350°F/Gas Mark 4. Using a 4-cm/½-inch round pastry cutter, cut out 12 pastry rounds. Re-roll and use the puff pastry leftovers if there is not enough to make 12 discs.

Place the pastry rounds on a flat tray, lined with greaseproof paper. Lay another layer of greaseproof paper over the top and then place a slightly smaller flat tray on top. (This will prevent the puff pastry from rising in the oven.)

Leave the pastry to rest for 20 minutes in a cool place before baking in the oven for 15–20 minutes or until golden. Remove and leave to cool.

To make the pea and mint purée, blend the peas in a food processor and add the garlic, extra virgin olive oil, mint, soured cream, lemon juice, salt and pepper. Process until combined. Scrape the mixture into a small container and place in the refrigerator.

Heat a non-stick frying pan until just smoking. Toss the scallops in a little extra virgin olive oil and season with salt and pepper. Add the scallops to the pan and cook for 30 seconds each side. Remove the scallops from the pan and set aside.

To assemble, place a small amount of pea and mint purée on each mini tartlet. Cut each scallop into 3 slices and arrange on top. Serve immediately.

Scallops with Serrano Ham

serves 4

2 tbsp lemon juice

3 tbsp Spanish olive oil

2 garlic cloves, finely chopped

1 tbsp fresh parsley, chopped

12 shelled scallops, preferably with corals

8 wafer-thin slices Serrano ham

pepper

Mix the lemon juice, olive oil, garlic and parsley together in a non-metallic dish. Separate the corals, if using, from the scallops and add both to the dish, turning to coat. Cover with clingfilm and leave to marinate at room temperature for 20 minutes.

Preheat the grill to medium. Drain the scallops, reserving the marinade. Thread a scallop and a coral, if using, onto a metal skewer. Scrunch up a slice of ham and thread onto the skewer, followed by another scallop and a coral. Repeat to fill 4 skewers, each with 3 scallops and 2 slices of ham.

Cook under the hot grill, basting generously with the marinade and turning frequently, for 5 minutes, or until the scallops are tender and the ham is crisp.

Transfer to warmed serving plates, sprinkle them with pepper, spoon over the cooking juices from the grill pan and serve.

Sweet Peppers Stuffed with Crab Salad

serves 8

16 pimientos del piquillo, drained, or freshly roasted peppers, tops cut off

fresh parsley, chopped, to garnish

for the crab salad

240 g/8½ oz canned crabmeat, drained and squeezed dry

1 red pepper, grilled, peeled and chopped

about 2 tbsp fresh lemon juice

200 g/7 oz cream cheese

salt and pepper

First make the crab salad. Pick over the crabmeat and remove any bits of shell. Put half the crabmeat in a food processor with the prepared red pepper, 1½ tablespoons of the lemon juice and salt and pepper to taste. Process until well blended, then transfer to a bowl. Stir in the cream cheese and remaining crabmeat. Taste and add extra lemon juice, if required.

Pat the pimientos del piquillo dry and scoop out any seeds that remain in the tips. Use a small spoon to divide the crab salad equally among the peppers, stuffing them generously. Arrange on a large serving dish or individual plates, cover and leave to chill until ready to serve. Just before serving, sprinkle the stuffed peppers with the chopped parsley.

Mussels with Herb & Garlic Butter

serves 8

800 g/1 lb 12 oz fresh mussels, in their shells

splash of dry white wine

1 bay leaf

85 g/3 oz butter

35 g/1¼ oz fresh white or brown breadcrumbs

4 tbsp fresh flat-leaf parsley, chopped, plus extra sprigs to garnish

2 tbsp snipped fresh chives

2 garlic cloves, finely chopped

salt and pepper

lemon wedges, to serve

Clean the mussels by scrubbing or scraping the shells and pulling out any beards that are attached to them. Discard any with broken shells and any that refuse to close when tapped. Put the mussels in a colander and rinse well under cold running water.

Put the mussels in a large saucepan and add a splash of wine and the bay leaf. Cook, covered, over a high heat for 5 minutes, shaking the saucepan occasionally, or until the mussels are opened. Drain the mussels and discard any that remain closed.

Shell the mussels, reserving one half of each shell. Arrange the mussels, in their half shells, in a large, shallow, ovenproof serving dish.

Melt the butter and pour into a small bowl. Add the breadcrumbs, parsley, chives, garlic and salt and pepper to taste and mix well together. Leave until the butter has set slightly. Using your fingers or 2 teaspoons, take a large pinch of the herb and butter mixture and use to fill each mussel shell, pressing it down well. Chill the filled mussels in the refrigerator until ready to serve.

Preheat the oven to 230°C/450°F/Gas Mark 8. Bake the mussels in the oven for 10 minutes, or until hot. Serve immediately, garnished with parsley sprigs and accompanied by lemon wedges for squeezing over them.

Clams in Tomato & Garlic Sauce

serves 6–8

2 hard-boiled eggs, cooled, shelled and halved lengthways

3 tbsp Spanish olive oil

1 Spanish onion, chopped

2 garlic cloves, finely chopped

700 g/1 lb 9 oz tomatoes, peeled and diced

40 g/1½ oz fresh white breadcrumbs

1 kg/2 lb 4 oz fresh clams

425 ml/15 fl oz dry white wine

2tbsp fresh parsley, chopped

salt and pepper

lemon wedges, to garnish

Scoop out the egg yolks using a teaspoon and rub through a fine sieve into a bowl. Chop the whites and reserve separately.

Heat the olive oil in a large, heavy-based frying pan. Add the onion and cook over a low heat, stirring occasionally, for 5 minutes, or until softened. Add the garlic and cook for a further 3 minutes, then add the tomatoes, breadcrumbs and egg yolks and season to taste with salt and pepper. Cook, stirring occasionally and mashing the mixture with a wooden spoon, for a further 10–15 minutes, or until thick and pulpy.

Meanwhile, scrub the clams under cold running water. Discard any with broken shells or any that do not close immediately when sharply tapped with the back of a knife.

Place the clams in a large, heavy-based saucepan. Add the wine and bring to the boil. Cover and cook over a high heat, shaking the saucepan occasionally, for 3–5 minutes, or until the clams have opened. Discard any that remain closed.

Using a slotted spoon, transfer the clams to warmed serving bowls. Strain the cooking liquid into the tomato sauce, stir well and spoon over the clams. Sprinkle with the chopped egg whites and parsley and serve immediately, garnished with lemon wedges.

4

Egg & Cheese
Dishes

Spanish Tortilla

serves 8

125 ml/4 fl oz Spanish olive oil

600 g/1 lb 5 oz potatoes, peeled and thinly sliced

1 large onion, thinly sliced

6 large eggs

salt and pepper

fresh flat-leaf parsley, to garnish

Heat a non-stick 25-cm/10-inch frying pan over a high heat. Add the olive oil and heat. Reduce the heat, then add the potatoes and onion and cook for 15–20 minutes, or until the potatoes are tender.

Beat the eggs in a large bowl and season generously with salt and pepper. Drain the potatoes and onion through a sieve over a heatproof bowl to reserve the oil. Very gently stir the vegetables into the eggs, then leave to stand for 10 minutes.

Use a wooden spoon or spatula to remove any crusty bits stuck to the base of the frying pan. Reheat the frying pan over a medium heat with 4 tablespoons of the reserved oil. Add the egg mixture and smooth the surface, pressing the potatoes and onions into an even layer.

Cook for 5 minutes, shaking the frying pan occasionally, until the base is set. Use a spatula to loosen the side of the tortilla. Place a large plate over the top and carefully invert the frying pan and plate together so the tortilla drops onto the plate.

Add 1 tablespoon of the remaining reserved oil to the frying pan and swirl around. Carefully slide the tortilla back into the frying pan, cooked-side up. Run the spatula around the tortilla, to tuck in the edge.

Continue cooking for 3 minutes, or until the eggs are set and the base is golden brown. Remove the frying pan from the heat and slide the tortilla onto a plate. Leave to stand for at least 5 minutes before cutting. Garnish with parsley and serve.

Oven-baked Tortilla

serves 16

4 tbsp Spanish olive oil, plus extra for oiling

1 large garlic clove, crushed

4 spring onions, white and green parts finely chopped

1 green pepper, deseeded and finely diced

1 red pepper, deseeded and finely diced

175 g/6 oz potato, boiled, peeled and diced

5 large eggs

100 ml/3½ fl oz soured cream

175 g/6 oz Spanish Rocal, Cheddar or Parmesan cheese, grated

3 tbsp snipped fresh chives

salt and pepper

slices of bread and green salad, to serve

Preheat the oven to 190°C/375°F/Gas Mark 5. Line an 18 x 25-cm/7 x 10-inch baking tray with foil and brush with a little olive oil. Reserve.

Place the olive oil, garlic, spring onions and peppers in a frying pan. Cook over a medium heat, stirring, for 10 minutes, or until the onions are softened but not browned. Leave to cool, then stir in the potato.

Beat the eggs, soured cream, cheese and chives together in a large bowl. Stir the cooled vegetables into the bowl and season to taste with salt and pepper.

Pour the mixture into the baking tray and smooth over the top. Bake in the preheated oven for 30–40 minutes, or until golden brown, puffed and set in the centre. Remove from the oven and leave to cool and set. Run a spatula around the edge, then invert onto a chopping board, browned-side down, and peel off the foil. If the surface looks a little runny, place it under a medium grill to dry out.

Leave to cool completely. Trim the edges if necessary, then cut into 48 squares. Serve on a platter with wooden cocktail sticks, or secure each square to a slice of bread, and accompany with green salad.

Tomato & Potato Tortilla

serves 6

1 kg/2 lb 4 oz potatoes, peeled and cut into small cubes

2 tbsp olive oil

1 bunch spring onions, chopped

115 g/4 oz cherry tomatoes

6 eggs

3 tbsp water

2 tbsp fresh parsley, chopped

salt and pepper

Cook the potatoes in a saucepan of lightly salted boiling water for 8–10 minutes, or until tender. Drain and reserve until required.

Preheat the grill to medium. Heat the oil in a large frying pan. Add the spring onions and fry until just soft. Add the potatoes and fry for 3–4 minutes, until coated with oil and hot. Smooth the top and scatter over the tomatoes.

Mix the eggs, water, salt and pepper and parsley together in a bowl, then pour into the frying pan. Cook over a very gentle heat for 10–15 minutes, until the tortilla looks fairly set.

Place the frying pan under the hot grill and cook until the top is brown and set. Leave to cool for 10–15 minutes before sliding out of the frying pan onto a chopping board. Cut into wedges and serve immediately.

Flamenco Eggs

serves 4

4 tbsp Spanish olive oil

1 onion, thinly sliced

2 garlic cloves, finely chopped

2 small red peppers, deseeded and chopped

4 tomatoes, peeled, deseeded and chopped

1 tbsp fresh parsley, chopped

200 g/7 oz canned sweetcorn kernels, drained

4 eggs

salt and cayenne pepper

Preheat the oven to 180°C/350°F/Gas Mark 4. Heat the olive oil in a large, heavy-based frying pan. Add the onion and garlic and cook over a low heat, stirring occasionally, for 5 minutes, or until softened. Add the red peppers and cook, stirring occasionally, for a further 10 minutes. Stir in the tomatoes and parsley, season to taste with salt and cayenne and cook for a further 5 minutes. Stir in the sweetcorn and remove the frying pan from the heat.

Divide the mixture among 4 individual ovenproof dishes. Make a hollow in the surface of each using the back of a spoon. Break an egg into each depression.

Bake in the preheated oven for 15–25 minutes, or until the eggs have set. Serve hot.

Devilled Eggs

makes 16

8 large eggs

2 whole pimientos (sweet red peppers) from a jar or can

8 green olives

5 tbsp mayonnaise

8 drops Tabasco sauce

large pinch cayenne pepper

salt and pepper

sprigs of fresh dill, to garnish

To cook the eggs, put them in a saucepan, cover with cold water and slowly bring to the boil. Immediately reduce the heat to very low, cover and simmer gently for 10 minutes. As soon as the eggs are cooked, drain them and put under cold running water until they are cold. By doing this quickly, you will prevent a black ring from forming around the egg yolk. Gently tap the eggs to crack the eggshells and leave them until cold. When cold, crack the shells all over and remove them.

Using a stainless steel knife, halve the eggs lengthways, then carefully remove the yolks. Put the yolks in a nylon sieve, set over a bowl, and rub through, then mash them with a wooden spoon or fork. If necessary, rinse the egg whites under cold water and dry very carefully.

Put the pimientos on kitchen paper to dry well, then chop them finely, reserving a few strips. Finely chop the olives. If you are going to pipe the filling into the eggs, you need to chop both these ingredients very finely so that they will go through a 1-cm/½-inch nozzle. Add most of the chopped pimientos and most of the chopped olives to the mashed egg yolks, reserving 16 larger pieces for garnish. Add the mayonnaise, mix well together, then add the Tabasco sauce, cayenne pepper and salt and pepper to taste.

Using a piping bag with a 1 cm/½ inch nozzle or a teaspoon, pipe or spoon the filling into each egg half. Arrange the eggs on a serving plate and add a small strip of the reserved pimientos and a piece of olive to the top of each stuffed egg. Garnish with dill sprigs and serve.

Egg & Tapenade Toasts

makes 8

1 small baguette

4 tomatoes, thinly sliced

4 hard-boiled eggs

4 bottled or canned anchovy fillets in olive oil, drained and halved lengthways

8 marinated stoned black olives

for the tapenade

100 g/3½ oz stoned black olives

6 bottled or canned anchovy fillets in olive oil, drained

2 tbsp capers, rinsed

2 garlic cloves, roughly chopped

1 tsp Dijon mustard

2 tbsp lemon juice

1 tsp fresh thyme leaves

4–5 tbsp olive oil

pepper

To make the tapenade, place the olives, anchovies, capers, garlic, mustard, lemon juice, thyme and pepper to taste in a food processor and process for 20–25 seconds, or until smooth. Scrape down the sides of the mixing bowl. With the motor running, gradually add the oil through the feeder tube to make a smooth paste. Spoon the paste into a bowl, cover with clingfilm and set aside until required.

Preheat the grill to medium. Cut the baguette into 8 slices, discarding the crusty ends. Toast on both sides under the hot grill until light golden brown. Leave to cool.

To assemble the toasts, spread a little of the tapenade on 1 side of each slice of toast. Top with the tomato slices. Shell the hard-boiled eggs, then slice and arrange over the tomatoes. Dot each egg slice with a little of the remaining tapenade and top with anchovies. Halve the marinated olives and arrange 2 halves on each toast. Serve immediately.

Chorizo & Quail Egg Toasts

serves 6

12 slices of baguette, sliced on the diagonal, about 5 mm/¼ inch thick

about 40 g/1½ oz cured, ready-to-eat chorizo, cut into thin slices

olive oil

12 quail eggs

mild paprika

salt and pepper

Preheat the grill to high. Arrange the slices of bread on a baking sheet and grill until golden brown on both sides.

Cut or fold the chorizo slices to fit on the toasts; set aside. Heat a thin layer of oil in a large frying pan over a medium heat until a cube of day-old bread sizzles – this takes about 40 seconds. Break the eggs into the frying pan and fry, spooning the fat over the yolks, until the whites are set and the yolks are cooked to your liking.

Remove the fried eggs from the frying pan and drain on kitchen paper. Immediately transfer to the chorizo-topped toasts and dust with paprika. Sprinkle with salt and pepper to taste, and serve at once.

Empanadillas with Cheese & Olives

serves 6

85 g/3 oz firm or soft cheese

85 g/3 oz stoned green Spanish olives

55 g/2 oz sun-dried tomatoes in oil, drained

50 g/1¾ oz canned anchovy fillets, drained

55 g/2 oz sun-dried tomato paste

500 g/1 lb 2 oz ready-made puff pastry, thawed if frozen

plain flour, for dusting

beaten egg, for glazing

pepper

Preheat the oven to 200°C/400°F/Gas Mark 6. Cut the cheese into small dice measuring about 5 mm/¼ inch. Chop the olives, sun-dried tomatoes and anchovies into pieces about the same size as the cheese. Place all the chopped ingredients in a bowl, season to taste with pepper and gently mix together. Stir in the sun-dried tomato paste.

Thinly roll out the puff pastry on a lightly floured work surface. Using a plain, round 8-cm/3¼-inch cutter, cut into 16 rounds. Gently pile the trimmings together, roll out again, then cut out a further 8 rounds. Using a teaspoon, place a little of the prepared filling equally in the centre of each of the pastry rounds.

Dampen the edges of the pastry with a little water, then bring up the sides to completely cover the filling and pinch the edges together with your fingers to seal them. With the point of a sharp knife, make a small slit in the top of each pastry. You can store the pastries in the refrigerator at this stage until you are ready to bake them.

Place the pastries onto dampened baking trays and brush each with a little beaten egg to glaze. Bake in the preheated oven for 10–15 minutes, or until golden brown, crisp and well risen. Serve the empanadillas piping hot, warm or cold.

Sun-dried Tomato & Goat's Cheese Tarts

serves 6

70 g/2½ oz sun-dried tomatoes in oil, drained and 2 tbsp oil reserved

1 courgette, thinly sliced

1 garlic clove, crushed

250 g/9 oz puff pastry, thawed if frozen

plain flour, for dusting

150 g/5½ oz soft goat's cheese

salt and pepper

Preheat the oven to 220°C/425°F/Gas Mark 7. Dampen a large baking sheet. Finely chop the sun-dried tomatoes and reserve. Heat 1 tablespoon of the reserved oil from the tomatoes in a large frying pan, add the courgette slices and cook over a medium heat, stirring occasionally, for 8–10 minutes until golden brown on both sides. Add the garlic and cook, stirring, for 30 seconds. Remove from the heat and leave to cool while you prepare the pastry bases.

Thinly roll out the pastry on a lightly floured work surface. Using a plain, 9-cm/3½-inch cutter, cut out 12 rounds, re-rolling the trimmings as necessary. Transfer the rounds to the prepared baking sheet and prick 3–4 times with the tines of a fork. Divide the courgette mixture equally among the pastry rounds, add the tomatoes, leaving a 1-cm/½-inch border around the edge, and top each tart with a spoonful of goat's cheese. Drizzle over 1 tablespoon of the remaining oil from the tomatoes and season to taste with salt and pepper.

Bake the tarts in the preheated oven for 10–15 minutes until golden brown and well risen. Serve warm.

Deep-fried Manchego Cheese

serves 6–8

200 g/7 oz Manchego cheese

3 tbsp plain flour

1 egg

1 tsp water

85 g/3 oz fresh white or brown breadcrumbs

sunflower oil, for deep-frying

salt and pepper

Slice the cheese into triangular shapes about 2 cm/¾ inch thick or alternatively into cubes measuring about the same size. Put the flour in a polythene bag and season with salt and pepper to taste. Break the egg into a shallow dish and beat together with the water. Spread the breadcrumbs on to a plate.

Toss the cheese pieces in the flour so that they are evenly coated, then dip the cheese in the egg mixture. Finally, dip the cheese in the breadcrumbs so that the pieces are coated on all sides. Transfer to a large plate and store in the refrigerator until you are ready to serve them.

Just before serving, heat about 2.5 cm/1 inch of the sunflower oil in a large, heavy-based frying pan or heat the oil in a deep fryer to 180–190°C/350–375°F, or until a cube of bread browns in 30 seconds. Add the cheese pieces, in batches of about 4 or 5 pieces so that the temperature of the oil does not drop, and fry for 1–2 minutes, turning once, until the cheese is just beginning to melt and they are golden brown on all sides. Do make sure that the oil is hot enough otherwise the coating on the cheese will take too long to become crisp and the cheese inside may ooze out.

Using a slotted spoon, remove the fried cheese from the frying pan or deep fryer and drain well on kitchen paper. Serve the fried cheese pieces hot, accompanied by cocktail sticks on which to spear them.

Peppers with Fiery Cheese

serves 6

1 red pepper, halved and deseeded

1 orange pepper, halved and deseeded

1 yellow pepper, halved and deseeded

115 g/4 oz Afuega'l Pitu cheese or other hot spiced cheese, diced

1 tbsp clear honey

1 tbsp sherry vinegar

salt and pepper

Preheat the grill to high. Place the peppers, skin-side up, in a single layer on a baking sheet. Cook under the hot grill for 8–10 minutes, or until the skins have blistered and blackened. Using tongs, transfer to a polythene bag, tie the top and leave to cool.

When the peppers are cool enough to handle, peel off the skin with your fingers or a knife and discard it. Place the peppers on a serving plate and sprinkle over the cheese.

Whisk the honey and vinegar together in a bowl and season to taste with salt and pepper. Pour the dressing over the peppers, cover and leave to chill until ready to serve.

Figs with Blue Cheese

serves 6

12 ripe figs

350 g/12 oz Spanish blue cheese, such as Picós, crumbled

Spanish extra virgin olive oil, for drizzling

for the caramelized almonds

100 g/3½ oz caster sugar

115 g/4 oz blanched whole almonds

butter, for greasing

First make the caramelized almonds. Place the sugar in a saucepan over a medium heat and stir until the sugar melts and turns golden brown and bubbles. Do not stir once the mixture begins to bubble. Remove the saucepan from the heat, add the almonds one at a time and quickly turn with a fork until coated. If the caramel hardens, return the saucepan to the heat. Transfer each almond to a lightly greased baking sheet once it is coated. Leave until cool and firm.

To serve, slice the figs in half and arrange 4 halves on individual serving plates. Roughly chop the almonds by hand. Place a mound of blue cheese on each plate and sprinkle with chopped almonds. Drizzle the figs very lightly with the olive oil.

Blue Cheese & Bean Salad

serves 4

150 g/5½ oz small dried haricot beans, soaked for 4 hours or overnight

1 bay leaf

4 tbsp Spanish olive oil

2 tbsp sherry vinegar

2 tsp clear honey

1 tsp Dijon mustard

salt and pepper

2 tbsp toasted flaked almonds

200 g/7 oz Cabrales or other blue cheese, crumbled

Drain the beans and place in a large, heavy-based saucepan. Pour in enough water to cover, add the bay leaf and bring to the boil. Boil for 1–1½ hours, or until tender, then drain, turn into a bowl and leave to cool slightly. Remove and discard the bay leaf.

Meanwhile, make the dressing. Whisk the olive oil, vinegar, honey and mustard together in a bowl and season to taste with salt and pepper. Pour the dressing over the beans and toss lightly. Add the almonds and toss lightly again. Leave to cool to room temperature.

Spoon the beans into individual serving bowls and scatter over the cheese before serving.